Arcana: Numerology, Tarot, and the Tree of Life

Sarah Wallin-Huff

Published by Sarah Wallin-Huff, 2022.

While every precaution has been taken in the preparation of this book, the publisher assumes no responsibility for errors or omissions, or for damages resulting from the use of the information contained herein.

ARCANA: NUMEROLOGY, TAROT, AND THE TREE OF LIFE

First edition. July 4, 2022.

ISBN: 979-8201381684

Written by Sarah Wallin-Huff.

Table of Contents

Introduction to the Deck

There are three major segments comprising a typical tarot deck; these are (in no particular order):

- Major arcana
- Minor arcana
- Court cards (considered a part of the minor arcana)

The major arcana are typically thought of as representing major milestones—life-altering events—whereas the minor arcana depict everyday happenings along one's journey. The court cards can be thought of as a combination of two elements; or, more precisely, how an elemental "personality" affects or is affected by the elemental "kingdom" in which it lives and over which it reigns.

In general, each of these three segments follow their own forward path, from birth to death, or from the start of the journey to completion. It is helpful to keep this in mind while interpreting the cards at any point. Whether it is a major arcana or minor arcana or court card that has been drawn, take note of where that card falls within its own segment's journey. This will lend a clearer sense to the card's interpretation in a spread: is this a fresh, new element; an in-between moment; or do we find ourselves at the end of a cycle, with new possibilities on the horizon?

An understanding of Kabbalist numerology and the symbolism of the Tree of Life may further enhance the interpretation of each card.

Much of what will be detailed in the coming pages has been taken from the insightful writings of Raven at www.corax.com/tarot and further built upon in my personal work with the tarot; I highly recommend Raven's website as a resource for your inward explorations!

One last note on duality. Inherent in each card is a set of dualities to be aware of. First, a card that is drawn right-side-up versus upside-down (what is termed a reversed card) symbolizes the difference between the original straightforward interpretation as opposed to the Shadow of that card. See the section on Reversals for more details.

One other duality to note is that of the Inner versus the Outer. Each one of these cards may be interpreted as energy being expressed between other individuals, or between different parts of our inner selves. A great example can be found in the Lovers from the major arcana. The Lovers are typically thought of as a harmony developed between two people. But that harmony may also be developed within our own selves, between our head and our heart. See the page on the Lovers for more.

As a self-styled "pagan atheist," I have never seen the tarot as a supernatural method for divining the future or taking command of otherwise natural forces. Rather, I have found the cards to be invaluable as a "mirror for the subconscious"—a way to better understand myself and my inner tendencies. I hope, as you explore the deck, that your relationship with yourself becomes richer.

My Favorite Spread

There is no shortage of creative and impactful spreads to be found on the internet, but allow me to share my own personal favorite. This spread is simple, can be used every day, and yet offers enough details and insight to satisfy one's hunger for inner knowledge.

- **Theme:** This card provides a sense of grounding, a center-of-balance for the question asked. It helps steer our intuition in the right direction and keeps us from being distracted with extraneous details that might not be pertinent right now.
- **Details:** Three cards that will help flesh out our understanding of what's going on "behind the scenes."

- *Head:* This card is representative of the detail centered on thoughts, ideas, plans, beliefs, etc.

- *Heart:* This card is representative of the detail centered on emotions, relationships, and other matters of the heart.

- *Feet:* This card is representative of the detail centered on the outward manifestation of things: action, ambition, goals, health and wealth, dealing with others in world, etc.

- **Advice:** What advice will help us move forward, now that we have the essential knowledge pertaining to our original query?

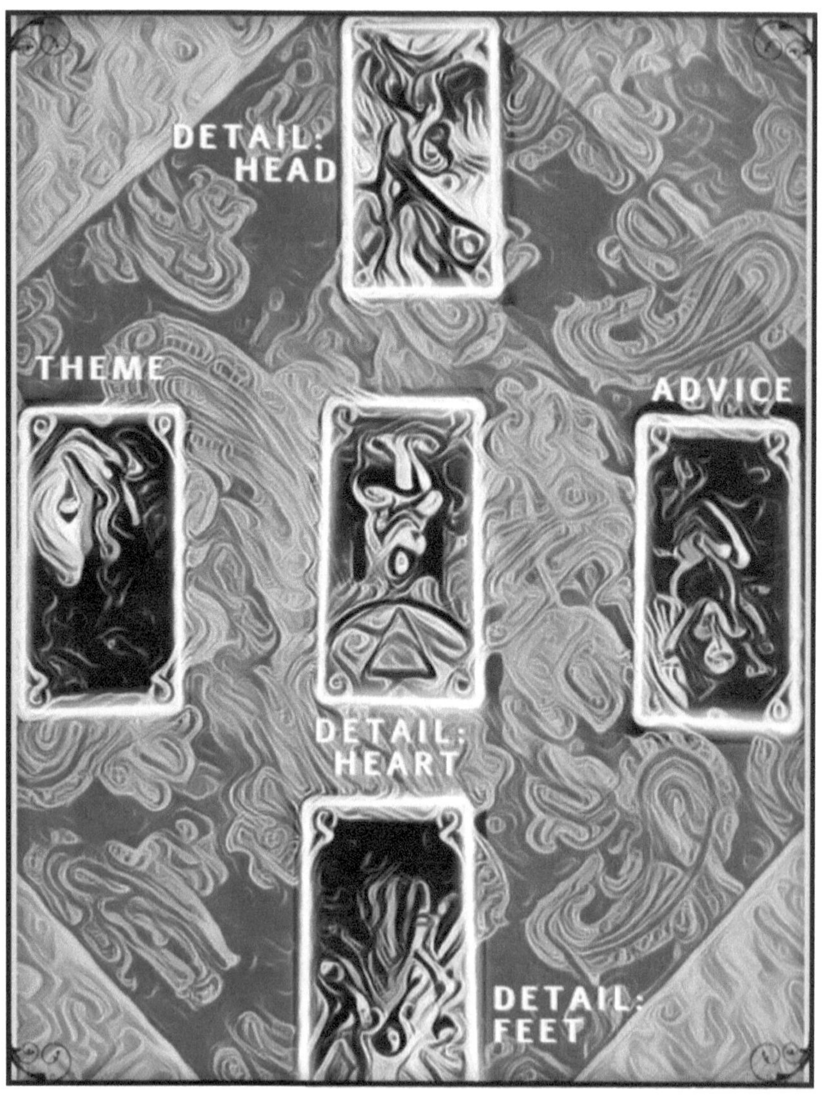
DETAIL:
HEAD
THEME
ADVICE
DETAIL:
HEART
DETAIL:
FEET

Reversals

While it is by no means necessary to work with reversed (or upside-down) cards, doing so does offer a further layer of clarity to a reading. I would **not** recommend using reversed cards until you feel confident in your understanding of the original, upright interpretations first. If the upright interpretation is clear, then adding a reversed interpretation to that foundation will make a lot more sense.

Drawing a reversed card indicates the presence of the Shadow of the original meaning; either the darker aspects of the card are taking hold, or the opposite of the original meaning is true.

A great example can be found in the Magician from the major arcana. Upright, the Magician takes all the elements from the Source and breaks them down to understand all their inner workings. The Magician can be thought of as the great scientist of the deck. They wish to fathom the elements and build upon the knowledge they get from taking a deep dive into what makes the Source, the Source.

Reversed, we see the Shadow side of this archetype.

- The darker aspects of the Magician's nature might include using their knowledge to deceive or manipulate others (or themselves).
- The blocked or opposing nature of this card might include an inability or unwillingness to seek the elemental truth of a situation.

Which interpretation is the "right one" will depend entirely on the card's position within a spread, the nature of the original question asked of the cards when they were drawn, and on your personal knowledge of the situation.

Meditate a bit on the card and the question asked, then trust your intuition; it will guide you to the answers you seek.

Overview of the Minor Arcana

Each suit of the minor arcana follows a path from 1 to 10, from seedling to completion. But the journey of each element is unique, its path unfolding according to its individual nature.

Each suit and its element are represented as follows:

- Wands = Fire: *energy and ambition*
- Cups = Water: *emotion and the realm of feelings or imagination*
- Swords = Air: *thought—the realm of ideas and the mind*
- Disks/Coins/Pentacles = Earth: *the material realm—health and wealth and other physical matters*

There are small differences found between decks, minor discrepancies in the symbology accrued as eons roll and as traditions evolve, and I'll make note of these as we encounter them. First, as you may have noticed above, different decks will freely label the earth suit as either disks, coins, or pentacles.

Knowledge of each element combined with a knowledge of numerology as expressed in the Kabbalist Tree of Life grants an extraordinary depth to the interpretation of the minor arcana.

Aces (1): Crown

Located on the Supernal Triangle, Center Pillar

The number 1 is the topmost point of the Tree of Life. It is the Source, the beginning, the holiest of holies.

The **aces** of each suit are the embodiment of the element in its purest and unaltered form. There is an innocence and naiveté to the **aces**, for they are the seeds of the element. As they travel down the Tree of Life, they will inevitably mature.

- Ace of wands *(fire)* is the first flame of an idea, a flicker of inspiration and ambition.
- Ace of cups *(water)* is the freshness of new emotion: new feelings that flow in new relationships or experiences.
- Ace of swords *(air)* is the breath of a new thought or realization.
- Ace of disks/coins/pentacles *(earth)* is the seed of material wealth or health, the starting point upon which earthly security may be built.

The reversals for each of these might either mean the element is blocked or there is an extreme or Shadow aspect to the card. (See the section on Reversals for more detail.)

Two (2): Wisdom
Located on the Supernal Triangle, Active Pillar

Two is a reflection of the Source above it. It multiplies the elemental seed by way of simple mimicry, like the early multiplication of a cell when it first splits into two identical copies.

- Two of wands *(fire)* is "Creativity"

- We are taking the first idea generated in the ace, and multiplying it and formulating new ways of combining notions into plans.

- *Reversed:* over-analysis, fear of the unknown, or lack of direction.

- Two of cups *(water)* is "Harmony"

- The emotional harmony found between two hearts that feel as though they are one.

- *Reversed:* This harmony is either blocked or manipulative. There is a lack of trust, disharmony, perhaps an emotional tug-of-war.

- Two of swords *(air)* is "Peace"

- Sometimes our thoughts feel united, but even when they don't and we are faced with indecision, there is a certain sort of peace there; a peace in not needing to make any decisions just yet.

- *Reversed:* Whatever this decision is, it is troubling our mind. There may be pressure to decide one way or the other, or some sort of stress associated with it.

- Two of disks/coins/pentacles *(earth)* is "Change"

- When material reality is multiplied, the nature of that reality changes, in big or small ways. This card can depict the yin and yang in balancing resources. Change is the only real constant in the universe. The sooner we understand that, the sooner we are able to ride the wave of Life.

- *Reversed:* We are unable to find our footing in this changing reality we find ourselves in, perhaps causing us to feel overwhelmed and off balance.

Three (3): Intelligence

Located on the Supernal Triangle, Passive Pillar

In **three** we begin to take apart the element in order to understand it better. There is a sense of scientific exploration inherent in **three**—building the understanding of one idea from the understanding of another idea. In this way, **three** is like a womb that nurtures these elements as they evolve. Processed wisdom or deductive reasoning is what is involved in this early progression of each element.

- Three of wands *(fire)* is "Virtue"

- When we stop to analyze what it is that truly drives our ambitions and energies, we develop a code of ethics or a framework of virtues on which we tend to build our future actions. This framework fuels our momentum.

- *Reversed:* Something is blocking our progress. Maybe it's disappointment or unexpected obstacles; perhaps we've lost sight of our personal virtues—the underlying reasons for why we do what we do.

- Three of cups *(water)* is "Abundance"

- A rich flow of familiar emotion, leading to more emotion like it. This may represent social joys of communing with friends.

- *Reversed:* The emotional unity we might normally feel being with others is blocked. Perhaps we are feeling lonely or competitive or jealous.

• Three of swords *(air)* is "Sorrow"

- An onslaught of unbridled thought can lead to sorrow; the mind can easily become overwhelmed with a torrent of ideas and take our emotions for a distraught ride.

- *Reversed:* The grief or suffering that too many thoughts can bring is healing. There is a sense of reconciliation, forgiveness, or compromise that often comes with a calm reconsideration of our earlier preconceptions.

• Three of disks/coins/pentacles *(earth)* is "Work"

- Like the framework of "Virtue" in the **three of wands**, "Work" is the result of building off the understanding of earth. Whether it is the realm of health, wealth, or outside relationships, when we gain an understanding of the mechanics behind these natures, we find that we are able to work with what we have in order to build something from these pieces.

- *Reversed:* Something is blocking our work efforts. It might be conflict with others or our own selves, ego, a lack of vision, disagreement... Either way, when we find ourselves unable to do the work we've planned on doing, it pays to take a step back and remember why we started the job in the first place.

Four (4): Kindness
Located on the Ethical Triangle, Active Pillar

At the heart of **four** is consolidation, stability, and structural integrity. The understanding we achieved in **three** gives way to the formation of a stable foundation in **four**—which we can further build upon. **Four** is also a symbol of community, of drawing people into our circle of loyal companionship.

- Four of wands *(fire)* is "Completion"

- *I have built a vision with my ambitions that draws others into community with me.* The "Virtues" that were discovered in **three** inspire others around us; in "Completion" there is a consolidation of everyone's energies into a place of workable goals.

- "Completion" may also be something as simple as fulfilling a small goal, reaching a milestone on our journey, or establishing a fruitful structure.

- *Reversed:* Discord, a lack of security or stability...something that blocks the completion of a milestone. Or perhaps the goal has been achieved but at the cost of losing our supportive community.

- Four of cups *(water)* is "Luxury"

- The element of water does not hold to a structure; it is free-flowing, and "Luxury" reveals this aptly. Emotion flows where it wills. Regarding our emotional relationship with others, their emotions are a reflection of internal processes, more so than a result of outward actions. In other words, while we can emotionally support others, we cannot explicitly make them feel how we want them to by any work of our own.

- *Reversed:* There is an effort to control our emotions or the emotions of others, to steer the flow of water in the direction we want it to go.

- Four of swords *(air)* is "Truce"

- Many decks depict this card as someone lying in a tomb. Ideas, like air, flow where they will. Too many ideas can cause sorrow (as it did in **three**), but there comes a point when we must allow this flurry of thought (whether entirely within our own mind, or breezing against other minds) to settle. It is often an uneasy or shaky truce; one stray breath could cause the delicate balance to tumble. But for now, there is a tentative truce of mind.

- *Reversed:* We cannot seem to let our mind rest or find even the most tentative truce. We keep chasing our thoughts and risk burning out from exhaustion.

- Four of disks/coins/pentacles *(earth)* is "Power"

- This is a peaceful sort of power, founded upon the stability that comes from wise material decisions, balance, and equality.

- *Reversed:* There is a fear of losing the modest gains we have, and we become materialistic and greedy. Or we are careless with our gains and spend indiscriminately.

Five (5): Strength

Located on the Ethical Triangle, Passive Pillar

In **five** we encounter the powerful forces of chaos, destruction, and change; perhaps the foundation we built in **four** is being tested... Similarly, the community we grew in **four** is now wracked with conflict or disagreement; the community is fragmenting into isolated individuals.

- Five of wands *(fire)* is "Strife"

- There are many voices, opinions, or ideas competing to be heard (this may be occurring within our own selves, as well as between others).

- *Reversed:* Here we are trying to avoid conflict altogether. Perhaps we don't voice our opinion and become jealous of others who do get heard; perhaps we are worried of being wounded or wounding others. Either way, the "Strife" that is present here risks not being dealt with effectively, which may cause it to continue bubbling dangerously under the surface. At the same time, it may be that this is one conflict we would be better off walking away from.

- Five of cups *(water)* is "Disappointment"

- When we are faced with emotional chaos or change, our hearts will seek an outlet where they can flow freely again. Water cannot stay trapped in one pool without becoming stagnant; it wants to move.

- *Reversed:* Somehow, we are able to move forward with our disappointment toward more forgiving waters.

• Five of swords *(air)* is "Defeat"

- In conflict with our own ideas, in our own heads, there is never any real "winner" in this fight. And so, comes a sense of defeat, a loss of personal ideals; we don't know who we are anymore if our own mind is in conflict with itself. It doesn't serve us to try to "conquer" ourselves; instead, it is better to love and accept ourselves as we presently are.

- *Reversed:* Our sense of "Defeat" is loosening. There is reconciliation, negotiation, understanding—all a result of acknowledging the mental conflict and choosing acceptance over stubbornness and despair.

• Five of disks/coins/pentacles *(earth)* is "Worry"

- Our material reality is falling apart—possibly through no fault of our own (recall that Nature is Change, after all). Regardless, when our plans stray from what we expect, this can cause a sense of worry.

- *Reversed:* In spite of the material change we have encountered, we choose to focus on solidifying what we have and rebuilding, looking for brighter opportunities ahead of us.

Six (6): Beauty
Located on the Ethical Triangle, Center Pillar

As the number that resides at the center of the Tree of Life, **six** is a place of harmony. This does not necessarily mean harmony with all things in all places; it is more in respect to the balance achieved between ourselves and our surroundings. It is the embodiment of the Scripture: *"I will have mercy on whom I will have mercy, and I will have compassion on whom I will have compassion"* (Exodus 33:19), implying that there may be those we reject for the sake of our own internal balance.

The elements are at home here, in purposeful and intentional harmony.

- Six of wands *(fire)* is "Victory"

- The conflict that arose in **five** has produced a definite victor. Whether that is ourselves or another (to whom we must acquiesce) depends entirely on the circumstance.

- *Reversed:* Either we are not the victor, or we are, and we wield it over our subjects. Ultimately, we feel we are not getting the recognition we deserve.

- Six of cups *(water)* is "Pleasure"

- The waters of **five** managed to flow onward and find pleasure here in **six**. Emotion is renewed, balanced, and harmonious. Nostalgia may also play a role in this sense of "Pleasure."

- *Reversed:* We may be trapped in memories, or otherwise not allowing ourselves to feel emotionally balanced.

• Six of swords *(air)* is "Science"

- The Scientific Method is a reliable formula for finding harmony among warring ideas. When we can focus our mind on truth and logic, we will find balance for our thoughts, which may help us find new paths forward.

- *Reversed:* We may feel stuck, unable to properly sort our thoughts out. Paralyzed, we risk avoiding the effort needed to seek out truth and answers.

• Six of disks/coins/pentacles *(earth)* is "Success"

- In spite of the chaos in **five** that caused us to worry for our material surroundings, we have overcome—perhaps we have rebuilt, or pivoted, or stayed the course, or otherwise adjusted our efforts—and we have found success in the physical plane. Because of our place of material balance, we feel capable of sharing our gifts with others. There is a sense of outflowing generosity and charity.

- *Reversed:* Perhaps we are not as assured in our success as we could be, and we display an imbalanced abuse of power or exude superiority over others because we are afraid of losing everything. We may begrudgingly offer help to others with an expectation of being paid back in return.

Seven (7): Force
Located on the Astral Triangle, Active Pillar

The world of **seven** is a place of anarchy and violent forward-movement, like the rapids of a stream rushing toward the ocean. It takes fortitude, persistence, and patience to follow through with our passions in the midst of the active force of nature that is **seven**.

- Seven of wands *(fire)* is "Valor"

- With the courage to face difficulty, we trust our ambitions and push through hardship. We hold our ground, defend our beliefs, and persist.

- *Reversed:* We are on the defensive, feeling attacked. Perhaps we have an aversion to hardship or are lacking in self-confidence.

- Seven of cups *(water)* is "Debauchery"

- When we link our emotions to objects in the physical realm—lusting after and tying our heart to events, goals, careers, belongings, and the like—moral corruption is the result. Life becomes illusory, tempting us to chase after material things that will not fulfill us emotionally.

- *Reversed:* We seek to escape this exhausting pursuit of temptations. In despair, we may let go of our own dreams and allow our emotions to be swept away in pursuit of the temptations the outside world puts in front of us.

• Seven of swords *(air)* is "Futility"

- Here we learn that more and more thought will not change our outward circumstances. Ideas are a starting place, but they alone will not change a circumstance. We may be hatching clever strategies or creating cunning deceptions in an effort to achieve our goal. But piling thought upon thought will be a futile exercise until we add decisive action to it.

- *Reversed:* All our strategizing may lead to self-deception and hostility. If we are too caught up in the whirlwind of plans to achieve our goals, we may forget why we are pursuing those goals to begin with.

• Seven of disks/coins/pentacles *(earth)* is "Faith"

- We take the material success that **six** brought us and invest it. After our hard work planting these new seeds, we must endure patiently as they take root and grow. Though the results are slow-coming, we know the rewards will be long-term. The harvest is not here yet, but we trust that it will come.

- *Reversed:* We may have procrastinated or otherwise wasted time in investing our seeds of success, meaning a lack of a harvest. Or we are impatient with the rate of growth, and we risk ruining the harvest by acting too soon.

Eight (8): Splendor
Located on the Astral Triangle, Passive Pillar

In the realm of **eight**, we observe the new landscape that has formed around us, accept it, and adjust ourselves to its influence, for better or for worse.

- Eight of wands *(fire)* is "Swiftness"

- Here we submit to the driving force of our ambition, without hesitation, and allow it to propel us forward!

- *Reversed:* recklessness, lack of direction, or a "digging in of the heels" to resist forward momentum.

- Eight of cups *(water)* is "Indolence"

- A lack of exertion, withdrawal, a resistance against activity or stirring up more emotion. We may simply be stepping back to observe our emotions as they are.

- *Reversed:* We find the willingness to move forward again. Or we are absolutely unwilling to move (we experience a total sense of avoidance, denial, and stagnation).

- Eight of swords *(air)* is "Interference"

\- Our thoughts are at a stage where they are interfering with our life. We feel trapped, negative, depressed, and we are hard-pressed to find the desire to break free of our self-imprisonment.

\- *Reversed:* In spite of the relentlessness of our thoughts, we dig deep to find the energy to fight against our prison. There are many coping tools we can claim and use successfully in this inner struggle.

- Eight of disks/coins/pentacles *(earth)* is "Prudence"

\- Our efforts in **seven** have paid off, and we have reaped a bountiful harvest. This surge in material wealth may further fuel our confidence; it is an outward reflection of our talent, expertise, patience, and commitment to our craft.

\- *Reversed:* Our harvest is mediocre or unprofessional. Perhaps we were unwise in our efforts. Or we may have been too hasty to put something out into the world, and what we have to show for it is not complete or worthy of our own truth.

Nine (9): Foundation
Located on the Astral Triangle, Center Pillar

Nine is a funnel of sorts, the place that receives all the lessons that came before it to feed the manifestation of Reality below in **ten**. It is a state of self-reflection, where each of the elements may rest and come to discern what they have learned so far.

- Nine of wands *(fire)* is "Strength"

- We built our framework of virtues in **three**, reached important milestones in **four**, faced conflict in **five**, encountered or became the victor in **six**, defended our accomplishments in **seven**, and allowed the momentum of our ambitions to carry us forward in **eight**. Now in **nine**, we stand tall in the sunshine of our past efforts. We defend what we have accomplished so far, in spite of the exhaustion we may feel after having already overcome so much adversity. We persevere because all of our work up to this point is worth defending.

- *Reversed:* The challenges we have faced to get this far are grinding us down, and we are having trouble finding the strength to continue standing.

- Nine of cups *(water)* is "Happiness"

- Looking back upon all we have felt and experienced, we find emotional contentment and satisfaction.

- *Reversed:* Disappointment and dissatisfaction color the view of our journey up to this point.

- Nine of swords *(air)* is "Cruelty"

- We have been unable to fight the self-imposed prison of our mind in **eight**, and our thoughts clutter even our dreams at night, stealing any hope of sleep from us. Perhaps our never-ending guilt or worry is what plagues our mind day in and day out.

- *Reversed:* On the extreme side of this card's Shadow, our thoughts are the root of unaddressed trauma or recurring paranoia, perhaps fueling a hatred toward our own selves that continues to make things worse. But if the Shadow is instead *blocking* this card's original meaning, then there is hope. Perhaps we are able to see the truth of what is causing our despair and use mindful awareness to begin reclaiming our mental health.

- Nine of disks/coins/pentacles *(earth)* is "Gain"

- The wisdom, patience, and expertise we leaned on to get to this point have firmly established our standing as a flourishing pillar of the community. We are stable, materially comfortable, resourceful, and we are in such a place of security that we have no qualms about helping others who may be less fortunate than ourselves.

- *Reversed:* Our success may be superficial; we may be trying to show off a prosperity to others that we have not yet earned. This comes across in the way we treat others in our material dealings with them.

Ten (10): Kingdom
Located on the Center Pillar

In **ten**, all of the energies and growth from the Tree of Life above are filtered and distilled through **nine** (self-reflection) into their most potent or mature forms. Here they appear as truths fixed in material reality. **Ten** is, at the same time, the end of this journey heralding the beginning of a new one.

- Ten of wands *(fire)* is "Oppression"

- We have taken on too many responsibilities; perhaps we were just so ambitious that we suddenly found ourselves shouldering more obligations than we can realistically handle. As is true of **ten**, the only choice we really have is to release this burden and start again with a lighter, more focused load at the **ace of wands**.

- *Reversed:* We refuse to let go; do we have something we feel we have to prove? The inevitable result will be burnout and collapse if we don't relinquish at least part of this load.

- Ten of cups *(water)* is "Satiety"

- Emotional fulfillment and security; stable and edifying relationships with others and self. At last, the rivers of emotion have arrived home to the ocean and are fully at ease with themselves.

- *Reversed:* Our emotional arrival is dysfunctional. Perhaps there are unaddressed disputes or a selfish withdrawal from others that muddy the waters.

- Ten of swords *(air)* is "Ruin"

- If our whirlwind of thoughts has remained unchecked and unacknowledged up to this point, we will be overwhelmed and collapse under the cruel sting of their cutting energy.

- *Reversed:* The flip-side of this card is hope for a new day ahead. There is nothing further we can do—struggle is fruitless—and all we can do is lie as though dead under the myriad cuts of our own undisciplined thoughts. But we also know there is a new beginning ahead of us. With the dawn on the horizon, we accept our current state of being and know that the **ace of swords** is just ahead of us.

- Ten of disks/coins/pentacles *(earth)* is "Wealth"

- The wisdom and patience we've employed throughout the journey of the pentacles has built for us such a stable platform in the material realm that we, our family, and our community may benefit from what we've built. "Wealth" is symbolic of legacy, permanence, and unshakeable security.

- *Reversed:* As with the **ten of cups**, it may be that our outward "Wealth" is superficial. There may be structural integrity missing beneath this facade, causing us to grasp at material wealth without really understanding Nature or ourselves. Consequently, jealousy and disputes with others will likely ensue.

The Court Cards: The Page

T he **page** represents the element of **earth**.

(Decks like the Thoth call this court card the Princess.)

Earth is a stable, unflappable sort of element. The **pages** are also the young children of the court, and they are shaped by their kingdom's element, albeit slowly. They are full of wonder, curiosity, and hope, and they remain generally unfazed by anything going on around them.

- Page of wands (*earth + fire*): This page gives ambition a place to feed and grow. But they must be careful they don't let that flame get out of control and burn them. They are an energetic explorer, eager to seek out all the possibilities of a situation or relationship.

- *Reversed:* We may feel disorganized, indecisive, or otherwise overwhelmed with all the possibilities around us. If the energies of this page are blocked, we may feel disheartened, as though our fires of ambition are fading for lack of fuel (the things that got us excited about our goals in the first place).

- Page of cups (*earth +water*): This page is surrounded by the fluid, ever-changing nature of their realm, like an island sitting stable in the midst of an ocean. They are a student of emotion, creativity, and faith. They are sensitive, playful, and imaginative. They can check to see if the current of emotions swirling about them presently line up with physical reality, thus enhancing our power over our own natural biofeedback loops.

- *Reversed:* The page may feel insecure with the rushing current of emotions around them. If left unchecked, emotions may overwhelm us and sweep us away in perceived wrongs, knocking us off our grounding.

- Page of swords (*earth +air*): This page is like a small plant that bends in the wind. They receive the thoughts swirling around them with curiosity, and, as a messenger, they are able to bring ideas into the physical plane. They are curious, alert, and quick-witted.

- *Reversed:* If thoughts get the better of them, this page will be tossed about by the wind. They may become rude, insulting, and defensive, while trying to hide their discomfort in the howling torrent of thought.

- Page of disks/coins/pentacles (*earth + earth*): This page is very comfortable where they are; they are entirely in their element, and they feel most at home here. They are resilient, patient, and at peace. Loyalty, practicality, and studiousness are notable traits of this page.

- *Reversed:* Earth is unshakeable; without a committed sense of direction, this page may find themselves lacking in ambition or discipline, remaining content to just sit where they are.

The Court Cards: The Knight

The **knight** represents the element of **air**.

(Decks like the Thoth call this court card the Prince.)

The occasional tarot deck has swapped the conventional elements of the knight and the king, making the king the representative of air and the knight of fire. The **knight's** character is that of enacting the **king's** will. So one could make an argument for the king holding thought in his hands while the knight wields ambition.

In my personal experience, however, I have found **air** to be the most telling element for the **knight**, as air is free-flowing and sometimes tempestuous. **Swords** being the suit for **air** also seems to fit well with the confrontational character of the **knight**. Air will effect change, driving the king's will forward (especially if the **king** is **fire**), just as fire will in the swapped scenario. But please feel free to assign your knights the element you feel best represents them.

Below are my interpretations of the **knight** as the wielder of **air** and thought.

- Knight of wands (*air + fire*): This knight is ambitious, tempestuous, and active. Thoughts feed and drive plans forward with ferocity and excitement. They are so confident in their ideas and beliefs that they charge ahead without doubt.

- *Reversed:* Reversed, this knight may become arrogant or volatile. Beware of impulsive, hasty decisions or reckless obsessions.

- Knight of cups (*air + water*): This knight is fluid in every way. Thoughts drive emotions into a tizzy and push the water's waves higher. He is often equated with the chivalrous knights and princes found in fairy tales: full of love, romance, poetry, idealism, and seductive charm.

- *Reversed:* The Shadow of this knight may reveal itself in insecure melodrama, vanity, and narcissism. Are we taking everything personally, or weaponizing our emotions against others?

- Knight of swords (*air + air*): This knight is completely in their element; they are at home here. Thoughts beget more thoughts, ideas bloom into more ideas. They are swift, focused, and decisive.

- *Reversed:* If thoughts become out of control, this knight may become aggressive, impetuous, and arrogant.

- Knight of disks/coins/pentacles (*air + earth*): This knight is patient and reliable. They enact change (as the others do) but slowly, trusting in the long-term success of their hard work.

- *Reversed:* This knight may become bogged down with earthly issues and have trouble moving forward.

The Court Cards: The Queen

The **queen** represents the element of **water**.

She is the mother archetype, she who nurtures the element of her kingdom and floods it with emotion.

- Queen of wands (*water + fire*): **Water** in the world of **fire**. These two elements are in a tenuous balance, as they are opposite in nature. When in balance, this queen is deftly able to influence ambition with emotional warmth (e.g., love, patience, mercy). Consequently, she can represent joy, enthusiasm, and passion.

- *Reversed:* When out of balance, emotion may flood and douse the flames of ambition, causing this queen to despair and give up on her goals. Or the fires of ambition may burn so hot that her emotional reservoir evaporates, leaving her ultimately unfulfilled in her pursuits while she succumbs to jealousy or spite.

- Queen of cups (*water + water*): This queen is in her element and feels most at home here. Her love and other honest emotions flow freely, uninhibited by anything else. She is nurturing, gentle, creative, and caring.

- *Reversed:* The extremes of emotion may be present here: despair and sadness, or capriciousness and moodiness. Are we being drawn into others' negativity? Are we being clingy or needy? Are we avoiding emotion altogether to save ourselves from pain?

- Queen of swords (*water + air*): This queen is able to master her emotions even in the face of turbulent thoughts. She is disciplined and wise. Her ability to balance thought and emotion grants her a strong sense of integrity and a commitment to her principles.

- *Reversed:* If the winds of thought stir her emotions into a sea of dangerous waves, she may reveal herself as bitter and critical of herself or others, believing the worst of a person or situation.

- Queen of disks/coins/pentacles (*water + earth*): This queen is as at peace, with a peace like the stillness of a lake resting in the earthen bowl of a valley. She nurtures the material realm with love and kindness. She is clear-headed (and clear-hearted), patient, caring, and generous.

- *Reversed:* Are we neglecting our earthly needs? Are we feeling insecure, self-conscious, or jealous of others? It is important to take care of ourselves, our bodies and our surroundings.

The Court Cards: The King

The **king** represents the element of **fire**.

(Decks like the Thoth call this court card the Knight.)

(Note that some decks swap the elemental identities of the knight with the king. See my thoughts on this under the Knight's introduction.)

The **king** is a force of stability and establishment. With wisdom and experience, he guides his kingdom. He is powerful and demands respect.

- <u>King of wands (*fire + fire*):</u> This king is at home in his element. He is passionate, confident, ambitious, and decisive—a natural leader.

- *Reversed:* He may distract from his powerlessness with arrogance or tyranny, stamping out dissent rather than leading with inspirational fervor. Are we feeling a failure to lead others effectively?

- <u>King of cups (*fire + water*):</u> **Fire** in the world of **water**: this king maintains a tenuous balance between these disparate elements. He manages emotions with quiet discipline and doesn't allow them to flow out of control, lest the fires of ambition and energy are extinguished. His shining qualities include diplomacy, wisdom, and sincerity.

- *Reversed:* When out of balance, reckless ambition may cause emotions to boil; or emotions may douse the flames of creativity. We may repress our feelings and our goals, and give up. Or we may become angry and lash out at others.

- King of swords (*fire + air*): **Fire** in the world of **air**. His ambition feeds on and further stirs up surrounding thoughts, but he's able to put both to good use by way of his experienced discipline, careful mastery of thought, and a desire for order out of chaos.

- *Reversed:* Lacking in discipline, he allows thought to drive his ambition toward recklessness or violence. Perhaps he is suspicious of others' intentions—his mind running on overdrive—but either way he may become conniving and unyielding in the pursuit of his goals, at the risk of letting his fiery nature burn out of control.

- Are our actions being done with discipline in careful thought, or are they reckless and hasty?

- King of disks/coins/pentacles (*fire + earth*): This king understands that the earth sometimes needs a controlled fire as a cleansing and rejuvenating element. But discipline, wisdom, and self-control are key to maintaining the material realm without utterly destroying it. He is a principled protector.

- *Reversed:* Ambitions risk burning down what is currently around us. Have we been taking who or what we have in our lives for granted? This king may express his Shadow in materialistic, exploitive, or corrupt ways.

45

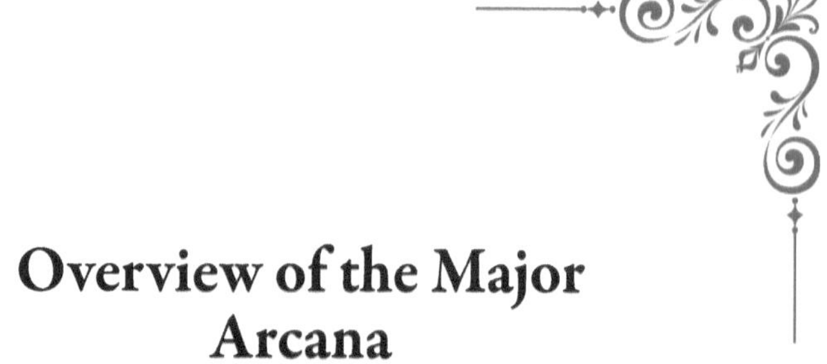

Overview of the Major Arcana

In the following pages I will lay out interpretations of the major arcana in accordance with their placement on the Kabbalist Tree of Life, as opposed to the traditional way of outlining the "Story of the Fool" numerically, from card 0 to 21.

Each of the major arcana fall within one of the regions of the Tree, or cross from one region to the next, thereby inheriting the nature of those regions or causing transmutations of energy. As we follow the Tree downward, evolving from the Source (1) to Material Reality (10), it is helpful to remind ourselves simultaneously of the numerological symbology we covered in exploring the minor arcana—the numbers which uphold the minor arcana are the same numbers that uphold the major arcana, after all.

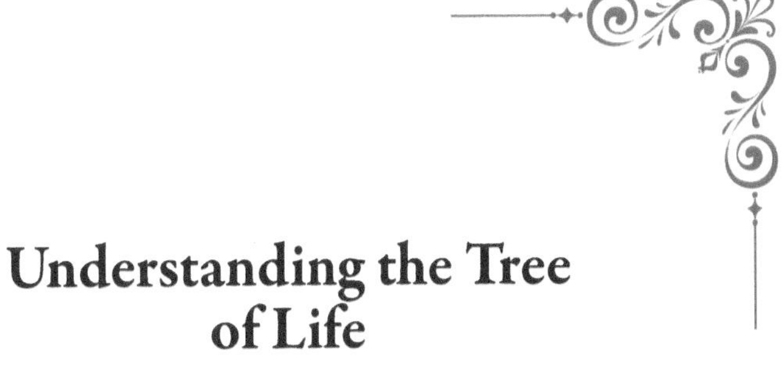

Understanding the Tree
of Life

The Tree of Life can be divided into three horizontal planes, moving from top (1: the Source) to bottom (10: Material Reality). And it can be divided into three vertical planes, each Pillar depicting one side of the duality (or the harmony of both sides) of attitude and reaction while in the specified horizontal plane.

The left side of the Tree is the <u>passive pillar</u> of "Severity." All numbers falling on this branch retain the following characteristics: passivity, intellect, restraint, science, entropy, allowing chaos to disrupt what it will. It is considered the "feminine" pillar because it waits as the fetus within is nurtured and grows until it is ready to be birthed. Here is where the numbers of 3, 5, and 8 reside. A general attitude of observation, patience, restraint, and judgment influences the cards that find their place here.

The right side of the Tree is the <u>active pillar</u> of "Mercy." All numbers falling on this branch retain the following characteristics: creativity, power, anarchy, ebb and flow. Nature is allowed to flow freely and evolve without restraint. It is considered the "masculine" pillar. Here is where the numbers of 2, 4, and 7 reside, and a general embrace of change or creation influences the cards that find their place here.

The center pillar is one of harmony and balance, the pillar of "Mildness." There is an <u>equilibrium</u> and sense of unity between the outer pillars here, where the numbers 1, 6, 9, and 10 reside.

The horizontal planes are laid out as follows:

- <u>The Supernal Triangle:</u> made up of 1 (the Source), 2 (creative power), and 3 (understanding). This is the triangle of Divine Consciousness, and it expresses the fundamental cycle of creation. The elements of this triangle simply *are* as they exist, and they are the pathway from the collective subconscious.

- <u>The Ethical (or Moral) Triangle:</u> made up of 4 (condensation), 5 (chaos and upheaval), and 6 (awareness and harmony). This is the triangle of intention. The elements in this plane are what motivate us in the ways we feel we ought to respond to that which affects us. In this plane, our inner virtues are formed and expressed.

* <u>The Astral (or Magickal) Triangle:</u> made up of 7 (creativity and anarchy), 8 (intellect and logic), and 9 (self-reflection). In this plane, our inspiration from the Supernal Triangle and our unconscious decisions from the Ethical Triangle become conscious action. This may be action to fight against an obstacle or action to submit to it, but either way the "magick"

of turning our conscious decisions into actuality is done here.

------ ⌘ ------

Finally in 10, tangible form and physical expression is given to the Source, as the result of its evolutionary journey toward the earth. Spirit has become fixed into form. Divine energy becomes physical reality, which then influences us as we start our next cycle back again at the top of the Tree.

Tree of Life: Passive Pillar (Feminine Energy)
Vertical Plane #1

Passivity, individualism, intellect, restraint, science, entropy, observation, and judgment.

- 3 - 5: Chariot
- 5 - 8: Hanged Man

Tree of Life: Active Pillar (Masculine Energy)
Vertical Plane #2

Creativity, power, assertiveness, anarchy, community, and evolution.

- 2 - 4: Hierophant
- 4 - 7: Wheel of Fortune

Tree of Life: Central Pillar of Mildness

Vertical Plane #3

Equilibrium, unity, harmony, and balance. A very spiritual plane.

- 1 - 6: High Priestess
- 6 - 9: Temperance
- 9 - 10: World

Tree of Life: The Supernal Triangle

Horizontal Plane #1: Subconscious Plane

The Supernal Triangle represents the cycle of Divine or Collective Consciousness, an expression of the fundamental cycle of creation.

The elements that form this triangle simply *are*. They exist in their purest forms, unaltered and unaffected by us or our surroundings.

- 1 - 2: Fool
- 1 - 3: Magician
- 2 - 3: Empress

Tree of Life: The Great Abyss

Between Planes #1

The arcana that cross the Great Abyss are those that reach down from above and bring the Divine Consciousness to our unconscious mind. It is the threshold between cosmic, collective sub-consciousness and the force of unconscious influence.

These include:

- High Priestess on the central Pillar of Mildness (1 - 6)
- Hierophant on the active Pillar of Creation and Anarchy (2 - 4)
- Chariot on the passive Pillar of Restraint and Entropy (3 - 5)
- Lovers, moving inward from the Pillar of Entropy to the Pillar of Mildness (3 - 6)
- Star, moving inward from the Pillar of Creation to the Pillar of Mildness (2 - 6)

Tree of Life: The Ethical Triangle

Horizontal Plane #2: Unconscious Plane

The Ethical Triangle is the place where intention and personal values are formed, that which dictates our actions to follow in the Astral Triangle.

The elements that form this triangle are our reactions to things outside of us that happen _to_ us, by which we learn and develop our framework of unconscious intentions. It is a **force.**

- 4 - 5: Strength
- 4 - 6: Hermit
- 5 - 6: Justice

Tree of Life: The Veil of Paroketh

Between Planes #2

The arcana that cross the Veil of Paroketh are those that transition from nonmaterial force and energy into physical, material form—that which can be seen.

These include:

- Temperance on the central Pillar of Mildness (6 - 9)
- Wheel of Fortune on the active Pillar of Creation and Anarchy (4 - 7)
- Hanged Man on the passive Pillar of Restraint and Entropy (5 - 8)
- Devil, moving outward from the Pillar of Mildness to the Pillar of Entropy (6 - 8)
- Death, moving outward from the Pillar of Mildness to the Pillar of Creation (6 - 7)

Tree of Life: The Astral Triangle

Horizontal Plane #3: Conscious Plane

The Astral Triangle is where our conscious decisions become action in physical reality. It generates tangible **form**.

The elements that form this triangle happen *within* us. It is here where the work of our consciousness is done to produce results in the physical realm. It is the place where our *individual awareness* blossoms, as a result from all the influences that trickle down the Tree of Life, from the Source and through the triangles and spaces that lie in between.

- 7 - 8: Tower
- 7 - 9: Emperor
- 8 - 9: Sun

Tree of Life: Bypassing Self-Reflection

Between Planes #3

Two cards transmit energy directly from the Astral Triangle to the final point of Reality in **ten**, *without* going through the self-reflective funnel of **nine** first.

These two cards are:

- Judgment, moving inward from the Pillar of Entropy to the Pillar of Mildness (8 - 10)
- Moon, moving inward from the Pillar of Creation to the Pillar of Mildness (7 - 10)

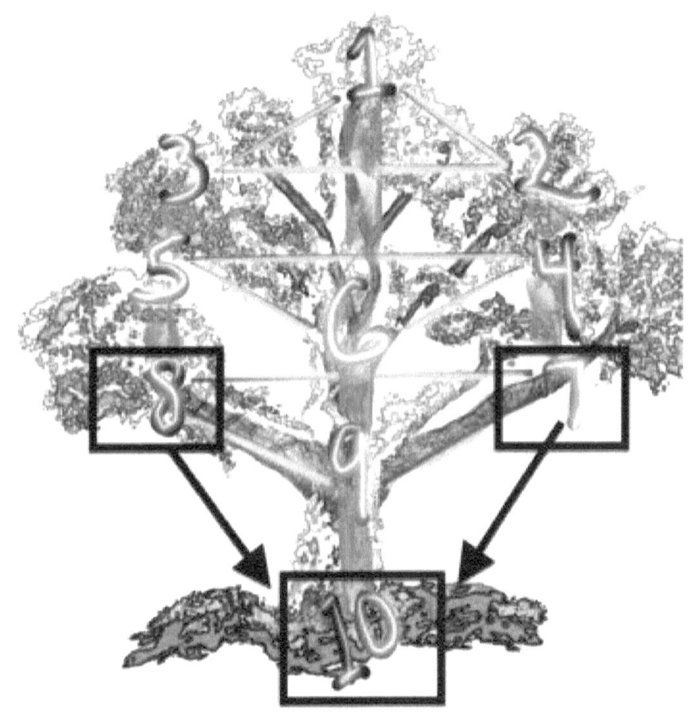

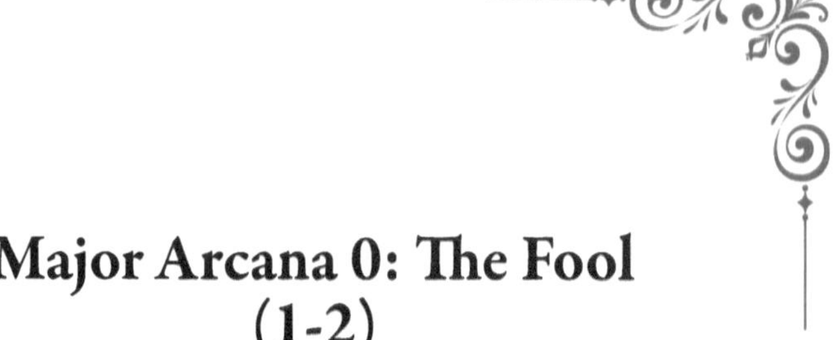

Major Arcana 0: The Fool
(1-2)

The Location

- the Supernal Triangle
- moves from the Pillar of Mildness outward to the active Pillar of Creativity

- escalation of energy; equilibrium-to-creativity

What it means

Starting at the Source of all things, there is a sense of purity and innocence that then imitates the Source (2) in an attempt to multiply and grow it, to become like it.

The Fool knows nothing else except what is received from the Source, so they have all the possibilities of the universe ahead of them. They are unencumbered by presuppositions, expectations, guilt, or anything of the like. They are a blank slate and eager to start their journey of discovery.

Reversal

A reversal of this card may indicate a hesitancy to move forward with faith in the unknown, or perhaps an overconfidence that becomes reckless and arrogant.

Major Arcana 1: The Magician (1-3)

The Location

- the Supernal Triangle (opposite of The Fool)
- moves from the Pillar of Mildness outward to the passive Pillar of Entropy

- escalation of energy; equilibrium-to-entropy

What it means

Starting with received knowledge from the Source, the Magician is the great scientist of the major arcana, the one who observes and studies the elements to really understand their inner workings and meanings (3).

Reversal

Reversed, we see the Shadow side of this archetype.

- The darker aspects of the Magician's nature might include

using their knowledge to deceive or manipulate others (or themselves).

- The blocked or opposing nature of this card might include an inability or unwillingness to seek the elemental truth of a situation.

Major Arcana 2: The High Priestess (1-6)

The Location

- the bridge across the Great Abyss
- on the Pillar of Mildness
- connects the two centers of the Tree of Life—the Source (1, or the purest of the Cosmic Sub-conscious) and personal, unconscious harmony (6)
- the first rung of the central pillar: from the High Priestess, through Temperance, to the World

Transmutation

- transmutes Divine Consciousness of 1 into the force of personal inner harmony in 6

What it means

The High Priestess is our connection to our inner world, our intuition or divine wisdom. She is a sign to look deep within for answers and understanding.

Reversal

When in reverse, the High Priestess may be ignoring her divine intuition, repressing inner knowledge, or feeling disconnected from the Source. Perhaps we are following the whims of outside voices, trying to please others, in search of guidance outside of our selves. We may feel aimless and risk acting before really understanding our true intentions, desires, or goals.

Major Arcana 3: The Empress (2-3)

The Location

- the bridge that closes the Supernal Triangle (equilibrium of energy)
- crosses *over* the Pillar of Mildness to unite the two opposing Pillars of Creation and Entropy

What it means

The Empress unites the two opposing reactions to the Source (as displayed by The Fool and The Magician): the Fool takes inspiration from the Source and imitates it; the Magician takes inspiration from the Source and inspects it to understand it as completely as possible. The Empress is the bridge between these two opposite reactions to Divine Inspiration.

She (like the courtly Queens of the deck) is the universal mother archetype. She symbolizes creativity, fertility, nature, and abundance, and she utilizes her feminine energy to nurture what she's been given and encourage healthy growth.

She alone is able to cultivate all approaches forward from Divine Inspiration (the Fool's path or the Magician's) and unite them under one common goal. She is responsible for integrating the various natures of our own mind so that we may be whole as we continue our journey down the Tree of Life toward the formation of unconscious intent and then conscious action.

Reversal

Her Shadow or reversal may be represented as either blocked growth (neglect, disharmony, stagnation) or an overbearing energy (becoming too controlling or too involved in the journey downward toward the Ethical Triangle so that we feel smothered).

Major Arcana 4: The Emperor (7-9)

The Location

- the Astral Triangle
- moves from the Active Pillar of creation inward to the Pillar of Mildness

- de-escalation of activity; creativity-to-equilibrium

What it means

The Emperor is similar in nature to the courtly Kings of the minor arcana, in that he exists to command the laws and oversee the structures that produce harmony across his kingdom. By way of the active *force* characterizing 7, his commands lead to the firm *foundation* of self-realization present in 9, which will give way to physical form in 10.

Reversal

In reverse, the Emperor's forceful nature may either be blocked (as in a noncommittal or ineffective leader) or expressing itself in the extreme (as in an entitled or tyrannical dictator).

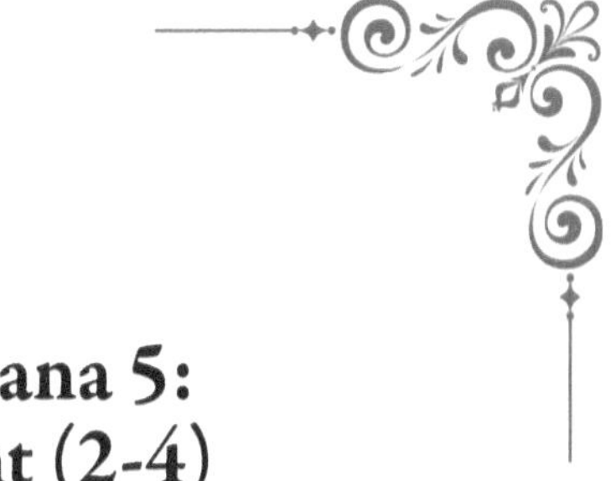

Major Arcana 5:
Hierophant (2-4)

The Location

- the bridge across the Great Abyss
- on the Active Pillar of creation and assertiveness
- connects the Supernal Triangle, starting at 2 (the perfect **reflection** of the Source—*not* the Source itself), with this "image of god" at the place of community in 4, in the Ethical Triangle of our unconscious mind

Transmutation

- transmutes subconscious power or wisdom (through mimicry of the Source in 2) into the force of personal stability and discipline in 4

What it means

The Hierophant is indicative of a priest who is able to bring the ways and will of god down to the people. He codifies received inspiration into a system of rules that is able to bring communities together behind a shared vision. Or, in other words, our subconscious reflection of spiritual matters crosses into intention, which influences our dealings with others.

Reversal

If he appears reversed, it may signify that either his reflection of heavenly things is marred or unclear, or that he may be abusive in his leadership role over the community. His role is only to *communicate* a heavenly ideal to his parishioners; what they decide to do with that information is up to each individual.

Beware of mistaking earthly definitions of heavenly things for the heavenly realm itself.

Major Arcana 6: The Lovers (3-6)

The Location

- the bridge across the Great Abyss
- moves inward from the scientific understanding achieved in 3 on the Passive Pillar of individualism to a state of total harmony and beauty in 6 on the Pillar of Mildness

- de-escalation of energy; entropy-to-equilibrium

Transmutation

- transmutes subconscious understanding in 3 into the force of unconscious inner harmony of 6

What it means

The imagery of two becoming one is an apt analogy for this card's movement down the Tree of Life. In passing through the Great Abyss, the Lovers take an observational knowledge of the Divine (garnered in solitude and quiet study) to a perfectly balanced place on the Ethical Triangle of unconscious intent—the plane where we become truly ourselves and from which all further, instinctual action originates.

Reversal

In reverse, the Lovers have difficulty achieving that balance in 6; there is a sense of disharmony, incompatibility, conflict, or selfishness.

Major Arcana 7: The Chariot (3-5)

The Location

- the bridge across the Great Abyss
- on the Passive Pillar of intellect, restraint, science, observation, and judgment
- connects the scientific understanding of 3 and brings it into the realm of 5 on the plane of mind and intention

Transmutation

- transmutes the subconscious understanding of 3 into the force of unconscious chaos or upheaval in 5

What it means

The Charioteer holds the reigns of a powerful vehicle, guiding two creatures of opposite colors. They must observe their surroundings and use intellect to guide their vehicle built by science and led by opposing influences. They are able to find balance between these two influences and lead them where they will. Their actions are a judgment they wield upon whomever they visit with this power; they enact change and/or destruction wherever they decide to go.

In other words, we move from a working, practical knowledge of a thing and use it to enact change in our physical world. May we take control of the reins and be willing to create chaos for our own benefit.

Reversal

A reversal of this card could indicate:

- something is blocking the motivation to enact change, or
- the Charioteer is losing control over their vehicle, and the warring creatures that power it are causing it to reel off course. Perhaps the Charioteer must go back to that initial, intelligent understanding of their warring influences to regain control and guide their vehicle where they intend to.

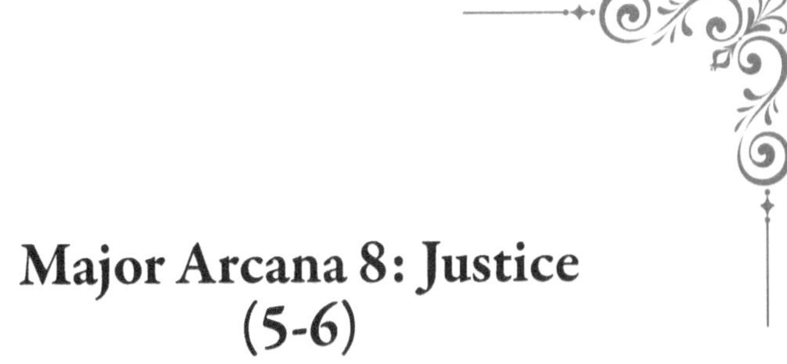

Major Arcana 8: Justice
(5-6)

The Location

- the Ethical Triangle
- moves from the Passive Pillar of observation inward to the Pillar of Mildness and balance

- de-escalation of energy; entropy-to-equilibrium

What it means

(Note: some decks swap the numerological placement of Justice in 8 with Strength in 11. I tend to prefer linking the observational character of 8 to Justice and the Yin-and-Yang nature of 2 [the numerological reduction of the number 11] to Strength. But as always, go with what seems right to you. Either way, each card's placement on the Tree of Life doesn't change, regardless of what number you attach to the card itself.)

Justice is karma, a great equalizer. They bridge 5 to 6, in the Ethical Triangle where intention and personal values are formed: that which dictates our actions that follow. They take the chaos and change they have been handed, figuratively push away others who may be involved (separating themselves from the community found in 4), and through this solitary reflection bring conflicting elements into balance.

Another way to think of this card's character is as the intention to disconnect ourselves from others in order to create balance and a conscious peace—creating a balanced intention within ourselves of who to let into our life and who not to (recall Exodus: *"I will have mercy on whom I will have mercy..."*).

Reversal

In reverse, this card indicates that there is an inability to find unbiased balance within ourselves regarding others. It could be that our emotions are getting in the way; perhaps we are too pressured to please certain people so that it prevents us from rendering fair and impartial judgments.

Major Arcana 9: The Hermit (4-6)

The Location

- the Ethical Triangle
- moves from the Active Pillar inward to the Pillar of Mildness

- de-escalation of energy; creativity-to-equilibrium

What it means

The Hermit takes the kindness, consolidation, and stability in 4 and moves it to the central place of harmony and beauty in 6. In this sense, he is withdrawing from the community of others in order to find his inner balance in solitude. There is a mood of letting go in this card, a sense of leaving behind the active, public life for a moment of quiet introspection.

Reversal

In reverse, perhaps the Hermit is unable to find that sense of harmony within and he feels lost or disconnected. Perhaps he is embracing reclusiveness and refuses to return to the community when it is time. Perhaps there is a feeling of profound isolation.

When in reverse, the Hermit must either have faith in the process of quiet introspection and wait to receive that inner wisdom he searches for, or be willing to return to society with the newfound harmony he has achieved.

Major Arcana 10: Wheel of Fortune (4-7)

The Location

- the bridge across the Veil of Paroketh
- on the lower part of the Pillar of Action
- connects the place of personal and communal stability in 4, and turns that essence into 7, the material form of conscious, creative anarchy

Transmutation

- transmutes the nonmaterial force of personal stability into the material form of creative anarchy

What it means

The Wheel of Fortune is a force of cosmic nature. It doesn't acknowledge a "good" or "bad" outcome to anything—merely the promise of change. The Wheel will turn, life will be turned upside down, for better or for worse; all the universe knows is *flow*: the eternal promise of cycles and seasons.

Reversal

In reverse, this card could be a forewarning of big changes to come, a reminder that life is full of changing seasons, or it could be a reminder to let go in the midst of difficult change and relinquish control of external circumstances.

Major Arcana 11:
Strength (4-5)

The Location

- the bridge that closes the Ethical Triangle (equilibrium of energy)
- crosses *over* the Pillar of Mildness to unite the two opposing Pillars of Creation and Entropy

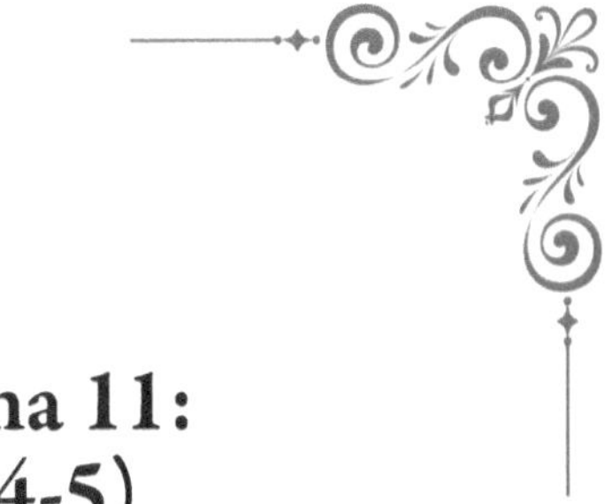

What it means

(Note: some decks swap the numerological placement of Justice in 8 with Strength in 11. I tend to prefer linking the observational character of 8 to Justice and the Yin-and-Yang nature of 2 [the numerological reduction of the number 11] to Strength. But as always, go with what seems right to you. Either way, each card's placement on the Tree of Life doesn't change, regardless of what number you attach to the card itself.)

Like the Empress closing the Supernal Triangle above, Strength closes the Ethical Triangle in parallel: the place of unconscious intention which subtly guides our actions.

Interestingly, these bridges are not where a thorough *blending* of opposites occur, but rather they maintain a delicate balance between two opposing forces— they oscillate between them and yet maintain a certain kind of equilibrium built on trust.

Typically, decks portray this card as a woman with some dangerous creature (like a lion or a dragon) held in her arms. The imagery implies that neither of these two (the woman or the creature) changes who they are to be with each other, but they manage to coexist because of the trust they have for each other.

So, in bridging 4 and 5, Strength is the space in-between community and chaos; we are skillfully managing our reactions toward others and to that which happens to us, without apology.

Reversal

In reverse, we may find ourselves incapable of finding balance between community and chaos and instead lean more toward one over the other.

Perhaps chaos is "rearing its powerful head" and we shy away from it, incapable of holding it close in trust. Perhaps we are experiencing self-doubt, vulnerability, or insecurity, and we doubt our ability to maintain a healthy balance with the chaos in our lives.

Or perhaps we have allowed the "beast to roam free", and we have lost control of our animalistic instincts. We react without thinking and act rashly without thought to the impact of our actions.

Either way, a reversal of this card may suggest a need to examine where the imbalance lies and to allow time to regain our sense of balance.

Major Arcana 12: The Hanged Man (5-8)

The Location

- the bridge across the Veil of Paroketh
- on the lower half of the Passive Pillar
- connects the unconscious upheaval from 5 to the patient awareness and submission of 8

Transmutation

- transmutes the nonmaterial force of personal chaos in 5 into the material form of conscious adjustment via intellect in 8

What it means

The Hanged Man is forced into exploring a reversed perspective of his current surroundings. He is physically restrained and unable to take any action except to patiently observe and reflect.

In the spirit of the Hanged Man we are moving from a place of chaos to a place of acceptance and observation.

Reversal

In the reverse, we may become impatient while being forced to wait. We feel stalled in our progress or stuck. Or we are afraid to make an important sacrifice and let go of our present attachments.

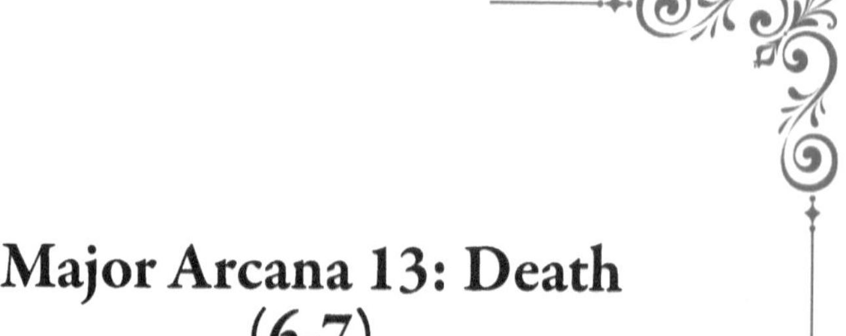

Major Arcana 13: Death
(6-7)

The Location

- the bridge across the Veil of Paroketh
- moves outward from the inner harmony of 6 on the Pillar of Mildness to a place of active fortitude against anarchy in 7 on the Pillar of Creation

- escalation of activity; equilibrium-to-creativity

- the opposite of the Devil

Transmutation

- transmutes the nonmaterial force of personal harmony in 6 into the material form of conscious anarchy in 7

What it means

Death is the opposite of the Devil on the Tree of Life. Both start at 6 in the central pillar, but (whereas the Devil arrives at submission and observation) Death moves outward to 7, the place of forward movement through anarchy and disruption.

This card is about embracing transformation, and acknowledging the end of something. Recall from the description of 7 in the minor arcana:

> It takes fortitude, persistence, and patience to follow through with our passions in the midst of the active force of nature that is **seven**.

So we are moving from a place of unconscious harmony to a new place where we must consciously endure with patience and fortitude as the winds of change toss us about and turn our lives upside-down.

Reversal

A reversal of this card could indicate:

- a stubborn resistance to acknowledge and allow change, or a desperate clinging to the past
- a complete sense of hopelessness causing us to falter and wilt in the midst of change

It bears remembering that change is the nature of the universe, and sometimes the best way forward is to acknowledge it, embrace it, and allow it to carry us onward to new places.

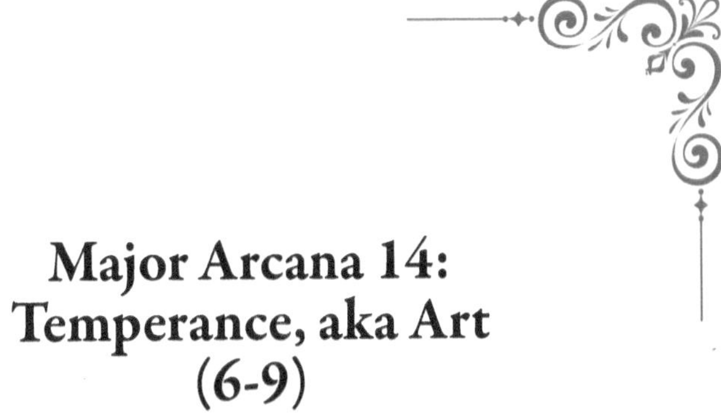

Major Arcana 14:
Temperance, aka Art
(6-9)

The Location

- the bridge across the Veil of Paroketh
- on the Pillar of Mildness
- connects the two middle centers of the Tree of Life—personal inner harmony (6) and the place of conscious self-reflection (9)
- the middle rung of the central pillar: from the High Priestess, through Temperance, to the World

Transmutation

- transmutes the nonmaterial force of personal inner harmony in 6 into the material form of conscious self-reflection in 9

What it means

The reason this card is sometimes alternately called "Art" is because of the nature of transformation. An artist takes the unconscious intention of desire and will, and—using an alchemy of training, study, creativity, patience, etc—they use skillful processes to mold that intention into its own Material Reality. Something that is of an artistic nature has received diverse elements of past influence and birthed them into something wholly unique and original. That is the essence of Temperance.

By receiving all of the disparate forces that have converged into the unconscious harmony and beauty of 6, the angel of Temperance uses the self-reflective funnel of 9 as an imaginative translator by which these prior elements might become manifest in a new physical form.

Temperance blends the *balance of intent* (6) into a *balance of physical form* through self-reflection (9).

Reversal

In reverse, this card might indicate an inability to move from intention to physical form or action. Perhaps we are feeling stuck in our current predicament and unable to realize creative solutions. Perhaps we feel incapable of manifesting meaning from our intentions. Or perhaps we resort to excessive, thoughtless reactions out of desperation and impatience.

The key is to remember that all Art takes time and patience to manifest. If we dig deep into our skills and innate creativity, we will be able to mold an answer.

Major Arcana 15: The Devil (6-8)

The Location

- the bridge across the Veil of Paroketh
- moves outward from 6 on the Pillar of Mildness to 8 on the Pillar of Entropy

  - escalation of activity; equilibrium-to-entropy

- the opposite of Death

Transmutation

- transmutes the nonmaterial force of personal inner harmony of 6 into the material form of conscious adjustment via intellect in 8

What it means

When looking at this card, we may either be the character of the Devil himself, or we may be one of his captives, depending entirely on its placement within the spread and in the context of the original question asked.

The journey of this card's energy starts in a place of harmonious, inward ethics in 6, and transitions to a place of passive action: observation, entropy (allowing nature to simply run its course), and acceptance of what is, as is the case of 8.

This implies that *something* is taking over our actions or physical reality (oftentimes this card is interpreted as a warning against addictive substances or behaviors). This *thing* is something that we ethically feel (or have felt in the past) harmonious about. We have willingly let this energy into our framework of values, and it is driving our actions—which are actions of non-interference and submission to obstacles. We are content to let nature run its course.

Again, whether this card is speaking of good influences or ill depends entirely on the context in which it is found. And, if we are the Devil holding the chains of the captors in this depiction, we seem to be very much in control of our own impulses.

Reversal

If we find this card reversed, it could be that our "addiction" is getting the better of us and keeping us from taking charge of our own lives in the way we want to. Or (in the blocked sense) perhaps we are at peace with this Devil, either comfortable with the passive place we find ourselves in, or on our way to discovering where we truly want to be.

Either way, it bears meditating a bit on our current relationship with this card when it appears.

Major Arcana 16: The Tower (7-8)

The Location

- the bridge that closes the Astral Triangle (equilibrium of activity)
- crosses *over* the Pillar of Mildness to unite the two opposing Pillars of Creation and Entropy
- interestingly, the Tower also creates a triangle with 6 at its apex, forming an "upside-down" union with the Devil and Death

What it means

Most decks depict a tower of some sort crumbling under a flash of lightning on this card. The idea is that, as we begin in the spirit of endurance amidst creative anarchy (7), we end up in 8–the place of submission beneath the winds of change in the physical realm.

Another way to think of this card's influence is that of a necessary destruction (of preconceived notions, of established habits, etc) befalling us due to outside forces, in order to bring us to a place of submissive observation where we can reevaluate our situation.

Something to keep in mind is that, like Strength and the Empress, the Tower oscillates or maintains an equilibrium between the two opposing forces of stubbornness and submission, without landing in the Pillar of Mildness. So, depending on the surrounding cards and this card's placement in a reading, we may currently be on one end of this transformation or the other—we may be in the stubbornness phase and must release our hold on the present, or we may be in a place of submission to our surroundings and must look ahead to the building of our strong tower with fortitude. Life is a constant balance of possible reactions.

Reversal

In reverse, we find ourselves resistant to the necessary and inescapable submission that follows the crumbling of our high tower. Or we are too comfortable in our place of submissive observation, and we are hesitant to start building our Tower anew. We are delaying the inevitable.

Perhaps we are doing everything we can to avert the coming disaster; perhaps we stubbornly close our ears to the truth in order to maintain our status quo. Or perhaps we recognize the destructive force of change and despair over the required transition.

Either way, it bears remembering that—in the Tower's case—change to our most dearly held beliefs or habits has come, there's no way around it, and the best thing to do is to come to terms with it and see where the light of Truth leads us next.

Major Arcana 17: The Star (2-6)

The Location

- the bridge across the Great Abyss
- moves inward from the multiplicative power in 2 on the Pillar of Creativity to inner harmony in 6 on the Pillar of Mildness

- de-escalation of energy; creativity-to-equilibrium

Transmutation

- transmutes subconscious, cosmic power into the force of unconscious harmony

What it means

The Star is a card of hope. It brings the creative power and cosmic possibilities from the Supernal (subconscious) Triangle and brings it to our unconscious mind and heart—to the place of total harmony and balance.

One might imagine looking up at a clear night sky, gazing long at the deluge of unobstructed starlight, and (by realizing both how small we are in the universe and that we are stardust ourselves) thereby become enveloped in a feeling of optimism in a vast world of cosmic possibilities. This card encourages us to look beyond ourselves and embrace the vastness of the universe.

Reversal

If the Star appears reversed, we may feel insecure, disappointed, or hopeless. It could indicate:

- we are too focused on our own smallness—our own little corner of the world, lacking the bigger picture—and we are encouraged to open ourselves up instead to cosmic opportunities, or
- perhaps we have spent too much time gazing at the stars in order to avoid moving forward out of faithlessness

Major Arcana 18: The Moon (7-10)

The Location

- bypasses the self-reflective funnel of 9, crossing straight from the Astral Triangle's conscious activity to the completion of physical form in Material Reality (10)
- moves inward from the active resistance faced in the anarchy of 7 on the Active Pillar to the Material Completion of 10 on the Pillar of Mildness

- de-escalation of activity; creativity-to-equilibrium

- the opposite of Judgment

What it means

Without a chance for self-reflection, this card indicates an impulsive move (an innate de-escalation of activity) from the creative anarchy of 7 to the home of Physical Reality at the base of the Tree of Life in 10.

In other words, Intuition becomes Reality. That which is found in our Shadow- or Dream-realms becomes our Reality; for if we'd had the chance to reflect upon these darker, hidden impulses, we might instead bury them deeply inside, hidden from the light.

Keeping all this in mind, we sense the full essence of the Moon—a calming release in letting go, of not struggling to keep our Shadow selves or subconscious impulses "in check". May our dreams guide us and our fantasies roam free.

Reversal

In reverse, we are perhaps still uncertain about revealing or acknowledging our subconscious selves. Or we are confused in the possible messages emanating from our Shadow-selves. The light of the moon is a reflection of the sun's light; the moon doesn't emanate its own light but reveals a modified, muted version of the sun's rays, and it can be disorienting.

Either way, illusion and uncertainty is covering our sight and darkening our path.

Major Arcana 19: The Sun (8-9)

The Location

- the Astral Triangle
- moves from the passive Pillar of Entropy to the Pillar of Mildness

- de-escalation of energy; entropy-to-equilibrium

What it means

The Sun moves us from humble submission under the outside forces of 8 to the conscious self-reflection of 9.

When the Sun is out, everything in its light is visible—thus the connection to both submissive observance and self-reflection. We can *see*, and our action (or inaction) in that light is conscious and intentional, as well as visible for everyone else to observe. It implies a well-deserved self-confidence.

Additionally, the sun's rays are life-giving for anything and anyone that soaks them up—an example of how self-reflection is an incubator for that which will emerge in the Material Realm.

Reversal

Perhaps we are worried about what we show to the outside world, fearful that too much sun will kill what we have; so we are reluctant to come out into the sunlight of truth. (This could apply to others in their relationship with us, as well.)

Or, just because we can see what's going on in the light doesn't mean we really *know* the context or meaning behind what we are seeing. We might be misinterpreting what we think we see.

Major Arcana 20:
Judgment (8-10)

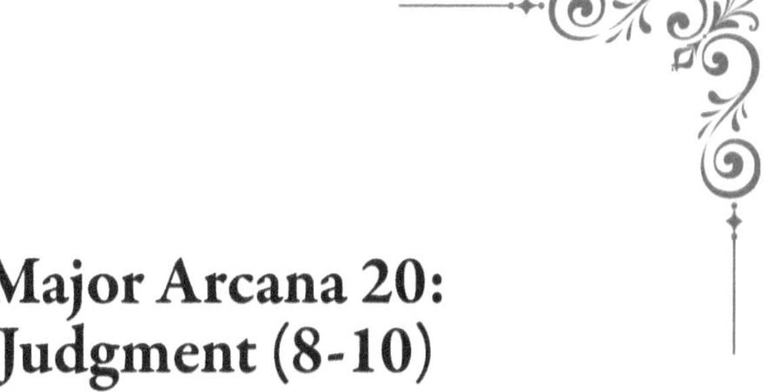

The Location

- bypasses the self-reflective funnel of 9, crossing straight from the Astral Triangle's conscious entropy to the completion of physical form in Material Reality (10)
- moves inward from the humble submission of 8 on the Passive Pillar to the Material Completion of 10 on the Pillar of Mildness

- de-escalation of activity; entropy-to-equilibrium

- the opposite of the Moon

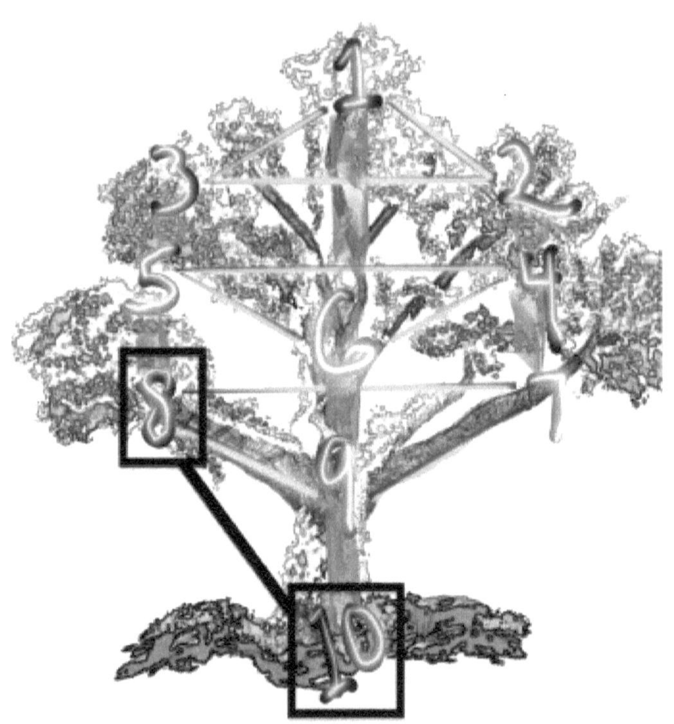

What it means

A great analogy for this card is the biblical story of Revelation: that at the blast of the angels' trumpets, the end of earth as we know it overwhelms us, and we are at the mercy of powers beyond our control. Like the Moon, there is an impulsivity to this card's transmutation—an innate de-escalation of activity, from the conscious submission of 8 to the home of Physical Reality at the base of the Tree of Life in 10.

In whatever circumstance we presently find ourselves, we are helpless to do anything but submit and adjust ourselves to the new Reality it brings us to. May we face this "new life" with grace, courage, and hope.

Reversal

In reverse, we may be fighting "tooth and nail", kicking and screaming against the inevitable tides of change. Or perhaps we are willfully trying to bring about an earth-shattering change when we and the universe are simply not ready.

Try as we may, there are powers in the universe that we cannot control, and for our own sanity it is best in these cases to yield our will and "go with the flow".

Major Arcana 21: The World (9-10)

The Location

- the bridge from Self-Reflection (9) to the completion of physical form in Material Reality (10)
- on the Pillar of Mildness
- the final rung of the central pillar: from the High Priestess, through Temperance, to the World

What it means

At last, we reach The World—all that came before, trickling down the various paths of the Tree of Life, is collected in the funnel of Self-Reflection (9), where it is distilled and takes physical manifestation in the Material Realm.

This is where we finish our current spiritual cycle and prepare for the next (starting back again at the Source). We have learned our universal lessons and have evolved the spirit of the cosmos to give it physical form.

By gathering all prior lessons above, in all the branches and leaves of the Tree, we are able to see the Big Picture of the World and let it shape our reality. We are able to see the application of all diverse elements as a part of The Entire Experience—and not just our own personal experience, but everyone else's as well, thereby gaining empathy for all fellow living beings.

There is a sense of absolute unity and harmony, inwardly and outwardly. We are *aware;* we are at rest, confident, and full of universal love.

Reversal

When in reverse, we somehow feel incomplete. Perhaps fear or self-doubt keeps us from fully embracing our Material Reality. Or perhaps we have many outward achievements but no real inward fulfillment—it is a false sort of completion focused on appearances or pleasing others.

Don't miss out!

Visit the website below and you can sign up to receive emails whenever Sarah Wallin-Huff publishes a new book. There's no charge and no obligation.

https://books2read.com/r/B-A-IACG-ZAJZB

BOOKS2READ

Connecting independent readers to independent writers.

Also by Sarah Wallin-Huff

The Kesher Archives
The Gospel According to Rachel

The Kesher Chronicles
Pursuit of Truth (Ultimate Edition)

Standalone
"Leviathan of the Ancient Deep": The Music's Story
Arcana: Numerology, Tarot, and the Tree of Life

Watch for more at https://SarahWallinHuff.com.

About the Author

Violinist/Violist, Composer, and Author Sarah Wallin Huff has been playing the violin since 1990 and composing since 1993. Sarah's music compositional style is what she calls "stream-of-consciousness" composition. She is currently a professor of music at Cal Poly Pomona, and published her first textbook, "History of Technology in Music," in 2019 with Great River Learning.

Throughout the course of her exploits, Sarah's literary writing has been a regular part of her creative life, beginning seriously in 1992. As she enjoys exploiting the abstract and the philosophical as a backdrop to everything she does, it is no surprise, then, how influential both her literary and music composition are to each other.

Read more at https://SarahWallinHuff.com.